MAGIC WITH SKIN ON

MAGIC WITH SKIN ON

MORGAN NIKOLA-WREN

Luminarium
PRESS

First edition
Library of Congress Cataloguing-in-Publication Date is available.
ISBN-13:   978-0-9985898-0-0
ISBN-10:   0-9985898-0-2

Cover art, "With All My Heart" by Catrin Welz-Stein
Cover design, art direction and interior layout by Madeline Crowley
Edited by Julia Guzzetta, Kimberly Ito and Alysia Nicole Harris
Author photo by Sara Shreves

Publication History: Act I, Scene I (formerly titled: Give Me More), and Act VI, Scene III (formerly titled: Toes in Tomorrow) first appeared in Writing Tomorrow Magazine, October, 2014. All other works are original to this collection.

To contact the author, email luminariumpress@gmail.com.

For Ryan,

> *who was pushing for this book*
> *long before I knew I had it in me.*

And for Robert,

> *who showed up to this wild party*
> *with more pixie dust*
> *than I ever thought possible.*

Thank you both,

> *for wrenching the magic out of me,*
> *even when I swear there isn't any left.*
> *I love you more than words can say.*

TABLE OF CONTENTS

reach into me
deep as poetry
tangle my veins
into calligraphy

ACT ONE

Slow your feet on the street that walks you home tonight. Never mind that the houses around these parts are all hunched together in identical, exhausted heaps. You'll know the one you are meant to find. There is a girl in it. Her slumped silhouette has the shape of the woman she could never quite grow into. And it quivers in the soft, almost holy glow of her window. She is breaking, you see? Practicing suffering like a sacred ritual. Because this girl doesn't know much about muses. And it's killing her, simple as a sharp knife.

Oh, she has enough friends to know how these things should be done. Friends whose muses are the bright and beautiful kind. These muses feed their mistresses bowls of Flawless Monologues in milk every morning. Serve them champagne flutes full of High E's, cold pressed. They have embraces that can melt their women into fluidity, swirl them into the most sublime gyrations across living room floors, and down halls. Most importantly, these muses stay; patient and steadfast, until the last song is strung together, until the manuscript unfurls itself into a magnificent sprawl of script across the desk. They stay for it all, brewing coffee, or honey infused ingenuity throughout. And their kisses taste like anything is possible. Or so she hears.

Hers has never gone in for that sort of thing— which is a downright tragedy, because he's got a tease in his lips that she would kill to taste, but never can. He'll never give her the chance. The satisfaction. The rush. Though he often comes close enough. And when he does, he hangs a second-hand smile across his face, snakes his hand around her waist—his fingers feel like a thousand perfect paintbrush strokes!—and dusts his breath across her neck like stardust. Each time this happens, every hair on her skin shocks itself stiff with genius. Genius and intoxication. She tells herself he comes so close because he needs her—Maybe it isn't need, exactly. But he must be drawn to her somehow. Why else would he place a necklace of notes so perfect she could never reach them around her neck with such velvet care and attention? Even if the songs do climb so high up her throat that she sometimes can't hear herself speak. Why else would he keep coming back to this place? Even if he does come flying through the door furious as King Lear's storm half the time.

What he's so hot-headed about, she can't quite say. Most of the time, he only stays long enough to calm down and eat half the food in her fridge. Then he's off again. Ever out of reach. He could bring this whole house, run ramshackle with all her wanting, to its full height again. Tall with all that they could be together. But he only ever slices his time here into moments. Just long enough for him to glance over her shoulder at the pen quivering in her hands; or crack open her bedroom door and watch her body throbbing, its movements wild to music she only wishes she'd written. His eyes are old theatre lamps, glowing warm against her skin. She can always feel his presence thick in the air around her, so that trying to push her pen forward, to move one more step across the music, is like trying to do so in quicksand. She hates herself every time she turns around to see him there. Hates that impossibly beautiful smile that spreads like sweet jam across his face—voracious amusement playing through his teeth, sharpened with all that she can never be. No words of wisdom or advice. Just a laugh, easy and flawless as decades of practice.

After that, he slips away, quick as the flick of a conductor's baton—and laughing all the while. He sounds like all the poetry she can never tie around her tongue, fading hopelessly into the distance.

But he always comes back.

Sometimes he even takes her to the theatre,
the circus, the concert halls. He likes the
sound of her soul battering at her chest, trying
to burst out onto the stage and drag her with
it. He likes tapping his feet to the torturous
rhythm. He doesn't bother wiping the tears
from her eyes. On the best nights, he pretends
not to notice them.

Look closer into that window. Watch her
tired face tremble, half with tears, half with
a candle's flicker. Even now, she cannot stop
searching for a way out of her skin and into a
life that fits all her fire.

I.

give me more

it's a night-shaped battle
as far as i can see
so give me dreams like
bruised knuckles that
no one dares to doubt
and a bloodstained smile
splitting open like
red curtains
before a symphony

give me more

it's grief like a sidewalk smashing
into my face post-fall over here,
so fill my mouth with
words to keep my teeth in place

and medicate me on
moments so resounding that
speaking is rendered pretty
much useless

give me life
not survival

it's been regret like a
crutch all year
so give me adventure that writes
its way through my story like
a lover, and a boy with a body
made of all my favorite
landscapes sewn together.

it's war like a neon
masquerade in these streets

so give me back myself

II .

i introduce you
to my tongue, and
it unfolds into
who i wish i was

who i am is
still searching for
the right words

III .

i wish i fluently spoke
the language of my prayers
half the time, i don't even know
what i am asking of God

only that i'm
an ever-growing tangle
of sacred sins,
only that there's this scripture
written at knifepoint
barely beneath my skin
and it's got me baptizing
everything i touch
in scars and sanctity

IV.

what i wouldn't give
to strip all this silence
from my tongue 'til
there was nothing left but naked truth

i want to say "broken"
in the simplest cry that
everyone speaks in the hollow of their throat
then open my arms
wide as i wish my lips would go

V.

my feet
may be anchored
to this place,
but i am begging
the wind to whip
my hair into a sail

i'm homesick
for a feeling
that has yet
to meet my fingers,
so, 'til then,
it bides its time
by tying my guts
into balled up
christmas lights flung
into a closet corner

VI.

i've got a soul stuffed full
of criminal wings unzipped
from my back
and feet fighting
to run wild beneath
all this celestial
weight

it's a struggle
to breathe through
so many dreams
they take up
all the space in my house,
if i'm lucky,
all this longing leaves
room
for air
in its wake

someone
planted centuries
in my soul. i get so
very sure of this
every time i try
to stretch
so much longing
across one lifetime

there is nothing that
leaves you feeling
quite so small
as having to shove
all this *being*
into your one allotted
body

VII .

trouble is
i wear my heart on
my words

so large
it chokes me
before any sound
can come spilling
into this electric air

VIII .

i've got so many
unsaid revolutions
crowding up against my teeth

not so long ago, i had
to swallow my tongue
to make room for them all

and i'm just now realizing
how much the innermost of me
tastes like fear

IX .

it's nights like this, when
your grief goes smashing
into the walls that i think of
those moments that curled your hand
so sea-shell perfectly into mine
my memory skips
at the velvet shock of your skin
and i wonder
how i ever managed to fit
so much rage into my fists

X.

there's a sea of unsaid
roaring through me;
shy as white lace waves on a shore,
but strong and stubborn enough
to carry ships on their back

XI .

something
in the dark of me
is begging to
throw open
its windows

ACT TWO

She is trying her best to keep him, of course.
Don't think for a moment that she is so
careless as to let him slip his way through her
fingers and away from this place for good.
She writes him letters—Isn't that what you're
supposed to do with a muse? And they're good
letters, too. All gall, no guard. She knows
better than that. She tells the whole story.

She's rending herself open, pouring everything
that will fall from her onto the finest paper.
And when only the best of her has stuck to the
ink, she folds each message carefully. Running
her hands over the creases with tenderness

printed into her fingers. Places them beneath the pillow in the spare room he sometimes occupies. Or in his dresser drawers, sparsely littered with the odd dance move or baritone voice.

The most daring of the declarations she slips under the floorboards, almost afraid of him finding them.

I .

you play chills up my spine
like perfect music
the kind i only know
half the words to

II .

i don't love you, you know
not yet
but i could
my stars, how i could

III .

whenever i find
myself swirled
into your presence,
these sickened smiles
you plant in my mouth
crowd out all the right words

but, oh,
how i lay you
across my pages
each night
and light declarations
up your

         every

   angle

IV.

i love you with a
caution so reckless,
it's almost feral

in secret,
i pry open your ribs
(like sacred church doors)

i lay my heartbeat behind one of them
for safekeeping

but i don't tell you which

V.

once you work your way
under my armor-thick skin,
you will find
a million love songs
swimming
through my blood
over countless arterial pages
of tell-tale ink
yes, the truth
wrings out of us all, eventually

VI .

i would sacrifice
days
of weeks
of months
of unwritten poetry
to soak up the soft of you

to feel our silken hearts
bloodied and muddied
and spilling their
exquisite grief

it raining down on the both of us
till we sprout words we never
thought possible on our lips

VII .

wrap me in roads
that never stop winding
let's take all our time
out on each other

i'll lace my fingers
steady through yours,
then press our palms together
'til our fortunes fuse into one

VIII .

i think someone
spiked my words,
'cause now,
i'm drunk on
love songs sloshed scarlet,
wondering how
your eyes became my
favorite music, and
when the walls
will stop
dancing around me

IX .

call me crazy
but i swear
you've got a
wild and ferocious love
sleeping
in your smile

X.

tonight,
when the moon
grows crescent horns
in the sky,
slip into something
more daring than naked
more honest than skin

i want to run my hands
up your childhood nightmares,
to feel your dreams
cradle my neck,
so bring me all
your grief-spattered mistakes
the ones that trail
blood and curses
on everyone's carpets

bring those hateful little yesterdays
that nip their needle teeth
at your heels,
keep you running your way
out of every embrace,
send you
reeling, wheeling past
every kiss that tastes
too much like truth

i swear, i'll weave myself
through the spokes
of your ever spinning
eyes till you go
dizzy with the knowing
that i am never leaving

'til your ankles stay still
long enough for those tiny
traps of teeth to realize
that nothing is so sweet to swallow
when you don't have to chase it down

maybe that's why you have yet
to stay when i tell you
i have no mind
to leave

i have no mind

ACT THREE

The pavement is pounding hot right through her shoes and against her feet. It is summer. Her hair clings in hot mats against her forehead. But she doesn't stop running. She can't. Her eyes sting wet with salt. Sweat soaks through the crumpled note in her fist.

It had been waiting for her on her desk when she got to work. And she didn't need to ask who delivered it. The love-struck stupor on the face of the new hire at the desk next to hers told her everything she needed to know. Her hands were shaking before she even took the cream-colored card between her fingers. Golden calligraphy sprawled luxuriously across it, pristine and poison—like arsenic poured into icing:

"I hope it was at least pleasant for one of us."

She ran out of her office without so much as an explanation—snatching up her keys, but forgetting her purse. And when the bus didn't arrive quickly enough, she ran the whole way home. Now she stumbles through the front door, the floor melting beneath her, his name charging hoarse out of her throat.

No answer.

He's gone.

She had him. All those times, she had him near as reaching. Right in front of her, in all his terrifying brilliance. And she wasted it. She should have kissed him when she had the chance. Framed his face firm between her hands before he could protest, or sneer, and drunk him in for herself—found out exactly what genius tasted like, glimmering on her lips.

Now all that's gone.

He's gone.

And he will not be returning. Just as the note had promised. He could always write in such splendid, greeting-card loops, no matter how much of a hurry he was in. And he was in a hurry. There are scraps of partially-formed inspirations strewn about, trailing from his room to the door, seeping themselves unreachable into the floorboards right this moment. The drawers of his dresser are half opened, the handle to one of them wrenched viciously from the wood.

She paces through the house, but her ears won't stop ringing. She is wondering when exactly he realized she was not worth anything he had to give. She wanted so badly to deserve him. To be the kind of magic with skin on that he would stay for, so promising that all his vibrant, beautiful life—damn, he literally made this place dazzle with it—could not help but splash technicolor across her every thought, every move, every endeavor.

Now, all she can feel are her guts curdling with the ghosts of everything she is not— clouding their way into the space he left behind. She wishes he had never once touched her! She'd have rather gone ignorant of the delicious rush of possible against her fingers. Never felt deep breaths of could-be, diving down her lungs, coursing their way out through her chest, coiling daring up her spine. She will never feel that again. Never hear his voice ease its way down the hall in flawless music. Never feel her bones tremble like violin strings at the sound of his footsteps. Never know just what his elusive kiss tastes like. Never know anything but this pain tying weights through her insides, twisting her in knots, wringing out all her tears, wrecking her into someone she doesn't recognize.

She cannot stop pacing through the house. Searching for him in all the quiet. Every time she walks by his room, the cavern in her chest yawns wider. He was magic. She could never stop being unsplendid, but at least she had him with her. All the powder-keg potential a person could dream of—sometimes just inches from her. Enough to keep her fingers branching out toward anything she could find blooming tepid between them. And now that's gone. She lost it. All that's left is an empty, ransacked room—And before she can tell just what she is doing, she is tearing through his trunks, his drawers, his closet. Dragging boxes from beneath the bed.

Maybe if she can find some remnant of him— his luminescence—in all this empty, she won't hate the house so much for not having him in it.

She is frantic to make all this misery, all this emptiness worthwhile.

She doesn't even notice them at first, at the corner of his writing desk. There, piled high in an effortless perfection—the kind that comes (came) to him simple as breathing—there they are.

Unopened.

She walks over to them. Takes the top envelope in her hand. Wonders why she thought it fitting to use that ridiculous wax seal. She always tried too hard. This is why he never read her letters. Even though he found every one of them. That's why he left. All of her trying made her rigid. Paralyzed. She could never make the two of them join, easy as paint hues. It was always a struggle. As the cruel fact sears the innermost of her, she digs her fingers into the paper and jerks her arms apart. It sounds like a soul tearing in two. Then three. Then four.

She is shredding each of them now. Every letter. Feeling the waste of it all split its way up her body every time one of them falls in scraps at her feet.

And they all do.

All of them.

All for nothing.

All of *this* for nothing.

I.

i wish all pain
left poetry in its wake

this one
just steals the light of me
turning corners of me
i never knew i had
heavy
and dark

II .

come back
and kiss
all this heavy
off my heart

III .

all that mad adoration
and you were blind to it all
i should have never
turned my body
to braille for your fingers

there was a time
when i found maps
to every familiar place
lined across your palms

now

your smile is just my
favorite ghost,
ever pressing
chills against the back
of my neck

IV .

as if hearts in
pieces
were not enough, you
ripped all the knowing
from our tongues, and
strung a broken
language
between us

V.

you live like a bruise
on my brain,
until i am blue-stained,
the color of
blood chilled away from
anyone's touch, and
a bandage abandoned
on the edge of my mind
waves in the wind like
a white flag, crying
mercy!

unhinge the echo of you
from my nerves!
this is an emptiness
too cold to carry,
my fingers are freezing
far past being able
to hold anything dear
again

VI.

there's an ocean-shaped
void in my chest
a thousand voices, swimming
roaring up between my ears
and a tongue
run dry of sound

is there a word for needing someone
to tell you it's never too late to
grow up all over again?

is there a word for wondering
how you're ever going to
tumble your way home
if you're not even sure
you've ever been there?

VII .

my heart's such a
stubborn beast
    beating
    striking
    fear into my future, for i worry
        no matter how many times
        i sew it back together
        with bloodstained thread,
        it will never stop making
        homes in your hands

VIII .

would it kill you
to carry my name
in your smile
the way you used to?

IX .

do not
call her fragile
simply because she
is in pieces

you'll never
know what it took
to break her

X.

there's an
extravagant kind of suffering
to her, tears
drip like diamonds from
her eyes, and she wears
her gloom like a
gossamer dress,
like she knows this
pain won't be around
forever to teach her
how she feels beneath it

ACT FOUR

Everything hurts. The colors outside are so
bright, they assault her eyes. The sun burns
like a scarlet stab in the sky. Still, she drags
herself down the street. She needs to be
anywhere but home right now. That house
is suffocating her with all its emptiness. She
needs a drink.

She cradles the mutilated letters in her arms.
All of them. Overflowing. A heap of ink-
stained innards spilling out of her. And she
does not care if they make a spectacle for the
passersby. She does not care. (The passersby

take no notice.)

She slumps onto the barstool like someone
knifed in the gut. Wearily, she lays her cursive
viscera down onto the mahogany. The scraps
flutter down and, for a moment, she wonders
what they would looked like baptized in
tears and spilled liquor. That's when she
notices it: All her dismembered declarations
strung across her eyes in a new, fragmented
simplicity.

She slides another stray word into place among
them. Watches years of misguided yearning
rearrange into something she can barely make
out, but wants to.

She asks the bartender if she can borrow a
pen, and she orders a coffee instead. Then
another. And another. Until the lights come
up and the workers are whisking brooms
across the empty floor beneath her.

She says she'll see them the next day. And she does. She brings her own pen this time, and she drains it dry. Her next five follow suit.

She writes as though every thousand poems can join hands in a collective chain, reach their way back into her 'should have done's, and pass one of them back to her.

She takes to bed each night, dreaming herself between sheets of paper, then wakes with ink in the blacks of her eyes, so that the whole world looks dipped in story.

Her story.

Her magnum mistake of a story no one will read.

Still, she writes.

The cabaret slips the most haunting songs through her window, and she writes.

She cannot find him in the stray boys she brings home with her across the nights, and still she writes.

The theatre down the road pours its stage lights over actors, painted and poised like exquisite marionettes, still she writes.

The city throbs lustrous with all the lives she would rend herself open for, and still she writes. She rages. She prays. She ponders.

And every so often, she tells someone a piece of her story.

Anything to make sense of it all.

And all the while, something deep inside her is finally beginning to uncurl.

I .

so hungry for adventure
i always used to
beg you
to weave your bootlaces
up your words
so i could taste every
land you'd
been to in your
kiss

a shoestring romance,
all we could afford
in the precious little
that remained
between your wanderings

and you may have had
a plane ticket for a tongue,
but you were the most

delicious travel expense
i ever spread
across my "i love yous"

carving jam-scarlet smiles
into my heart
until you'd dug a hole
just your shape

i didn't even notice the
empty space until you
were a sea away and i
was still sky high,
pocketing all that
freezing air in
my chest

the terrible truth
is anything

can look like love if
you've got enough lonely
in your eyes

II .

today, the door
swings open and
spills shadows like yours
across the floor

today, every voice
that sneaks up behind me
is dipped in your laugh

and i can't help
but hate myself for it

you stabbed the air
with my name, like it
was poison, like you
couldn't wait to spit it
out of your mouth, like you
never asked for it in the
first place, like you

never draped it
across a voice soft
as candlelight

and here i am,
still insisting every dream that
does not hand you
over to me
is a mistake

III .

i think i spent
so long telling myself
that love was madness
because i was so scared
of leaving your
straitjacket embrace

that's what you call
committed

IV .

you tossed me
your hand-me-down love
like it was an old sweater
never really meant for me
but all i could afford
at the time

so, it always hung awkward
on my shoulders
gaped far from my form
a web of complications
knitted, knotted into something that
could have been warm if you'd just
clung to me,
if i'd just grown into you
or into something you could have
wrapped yourself around
maybe then
i wouldn't have tried to

fill up the empty space with
all the wrong people
and maybe you wouldn't have
found yourself splayed
across a stranger's couch

V.

mine is a wild beauty
pearl claws in its smile

you'll know me
the moment i
set my empty
loose in this place

i've got
tired bramble for hair,
and my eyes
are feral's favorite color

i'm an entire
bestiary trapped in
a body, but no one
can find a name for me

nonetheless, i'll shoot
the bow of my lip
across the room and skewer
your longing with my kiss

VI.

i'll bet your kiss tastes
    like walking two miles
        just to buy me a drink

i think i have a
    separate heart for
        every love that's ever
            grown inside me, so

pour me a glass
    of your favorite grief

let me take on
    the empty that fills you

VII .

build me a summer house
in the gutters of your story

this vacant sadness
turns down my mouth like
a guest room bed you're
welcome to

though we both know
you won't be sticking
around

you'll never
taste
like home,

not the way he did

VIII .

my name rattles desperate
against your teeth

and yet

no matter how many times
it rides your voice
into the thick warmth
of this room
i lay
my head on your chest

                          after

and i swear,
i can hear a truer
shade of myself swallowed
down your throat and
banging your chest inside out
for an escape

i shed odd socks and
spare toothbrushes around your
house like old skin

i tell myself
i am becoming
something raw,

       pink and beautiful

but i cannot shake this fear
that i am losing

                    myself

            piece

                      by

     piece

IX .

if it were easy as
sliding off clothing, then
this silicon city would
have memorized
every inch of me
climbed its eyes
up a detailed count
of vertebrae, measured
the naked, cellulite sway
of my hips, noted
the ungraceful tremble of
my thighs, breasts
and stomach

if it were simple as
shedding skin, my flesh
would have fallen like
peels of fruit
at my feet

but the truth of me is
buried so much deeper
than blood, and every day
is a fight to share
my secrets with myself

X .

my God claims
the shape of my
body around me
even when
the only prayers i've got
are baseball bats, swinging livid,
He is still tattooed
onto each face
that drives me home
when i drink myself into
saturday night remnants

and i worry you want
words clean as sunday best,
all these big questions
pleated against the inside of my cheek
to make room for starched
simple answers, double windsor
one-sentence solutions

but i'm tasting
a different scripture here,
a testament to the kind
of truth you pull out from
under bloodied fingernails,
and a God who's not afraid
for you to find Him
in heaps of curses

XI .

give me a year
and i'll be proud
to recognize myself

for now
i am busy unbecoming
all the mistakes
i swore i would never
melt into

"waste" seems
such a cruel word for it
but what else do you call
all this time spent being
a stranger to your spirit?

XII .

i have let far too many boys
slide into me because
they were not at home
in their own skin

XIII .

the next time you come at me,
with charm in your eyes
and a throat full of
"would never hurt you,"
i'll remember that i'm just
a mistake your memory
couldn't carry, and you're
just an apology i'll never
hear the air explode into,
a double-jointed voice
and a snake oil smile—
so, scrub your shadow
from my front door
don't sell me
a knock-off
love i don't need

ACT FIVE

She is collecting pens like they are long-lost fingers. Spilling ink—easy as blood and twice as alive. It is all she does anymore. She didn't bother returning to work after he left. Half of her didn't feel like getting up in the morning. The other half wasn't going to wait to be told not to come back after pulling a stunt like running off with no warning, or even a phone call. So, these pages are all she has now.

She is courting herself. Getting to know the twists and turns of her. Intimately. The way you can only do when you have been shattered. Running your hands up every small piece of you before you it back into place—or even somewhere entirely different. Because it feels good to remind yourself that some changes are still within your control.

She has been pouring over her pages for weeks—months—now. Every spare minute spent tracing all the years that stretch behind her in a blurry handwriting that costs her almost every night's sleep.

She has forgotten what day it is. She is tucked away in her bedroom, hunched so far over the desk that she doesn't even notice him spread languid and luminous across her doorway. He has to clear his throat, the way an orchestra tunes before a performance. Then her hand freezes.

She feels a tremor in her throat, but hears no sound. Her "hello" flits frantic over her tongue, but she manages, at last, to iron it out of her mouth into composure. She wonders how she managed to forget how truly beautiful he was. She sees the upturned floorboard inches behind his feet. She wonders how she could have not heard him come in. Not heard him go searching for spare love tokens all this while. And when he sculpts the question, "You miss me?" on his lips, the whole house goes magical-silent. Like the second that's caught between a performance and raucous applause.

Had she really thought it would be so simple to be rid of him? That a being so gifted in dealing the unreachable and intangible would never slide his way back into her life? No, he's been dancing up her dreams all the while. Of course, he's back here now, gliding across the threadbare rugs toward her.

Her heart rushes blood through her chest, down her arms, crashing like waves into her palms, laid flat against the table. She presses them down, stands—her legs wobbling beneath her—and swims across the room to him.

When his hand snakes silken around her waist, she swears her spine's been wired electric, just waiting for this moment. She gathers up all the right words behind her teeth. Those sharp send-offs she churned off her piston tongue so many times. (She has rehearsed this scenario over and over.) She feels them, lined up eager against her lips, and she opens her mouth.

She opens her mouth.

And he is pressing his lips against hers at last.

She gasps.

She collapses her back into a curve against his arms.

She drinks him in.

And he tastes like every word that has yet to be invented.

When she pins a small sob to the back of her throat, he laughs, but she doesn't care.

She is weaving her hands through his hair like spun gold, her mouth swirling with a delirious creation—something to say. Something entirely new. Something no one has ever thought to fashion, and it's rushing over her very own tongue. It's hers! She's about to swallow it safe inside her. Her heart is opening wide enough to catch all she will do—all she will be—when it dives down her throat. All that misery. All that searching and now, all those dreams are hers, dancing over her lips! They're thinning against her tongue like fog. They're drowning in a bored sigh. And suddenly, he is before her eyes again, and she is choking on empty air.

"I knew you missed me." His words are satisfaction dipped in a velvet yawn.

Damn it all, even when he oozes disinterest, he sounds angelic. His smile's shaped exactly like an aria. Even his shrugs are a dance. An ancient and sacred grace shifting over his shoulders, so that she almost thanks him for the way her chest pangs with frantic regret when he slides out her door.

This time, she sees him go. Quick as a dream dissolving in the morning, but she sees it. He's tossing one last cyanide-sweet grin over his shoulder before the doorway swallows him and all his magic—all his astounding being lost once again. Her mouth is empty now. No words. No ecstatic tastes. But she does not run after him. Half of her spirit is chasing him down the street. And her mind is scrambling to catch up to it all. Still, she stays where she is.

There is nothing she can do to stop him.

Not so long ago, this would have yanked
out all the strength from her in an instant—
though make no mistake, when he sliced their
kiss in two, it felt as if he'd ripped out all her
teeth in the process. But she is still standing
this time.

Even though she walked right back into all his
perfect poison.

Even though all she's got to show for this
misery are two strands of his hair laced small
and sickly between her fingers.

Still, she's standing.

I.

your kiss
was a punch to my plans
now, i spit love songs
like broken teeth

II .

no,
i wouldn't call you
a monster
just a nightmare
dressed as a man
the kind where you can't
stop yourself
from falling

III .

i cannot say when
the no
fell out of my words

only that i am ashamed
of the empty
space it left behind

and how just anything
can coax
its way into there
now

now
the question jack saws
through this night-still room

"where did i leave my fire?"

IV .

you were
the most beautiful lie
i ever pinned
to my lips

V.

your kiss is like honey
just not the way i'd
come to expect:

i can't ever decide how
i feel about the taste
but heavens,
how it sticks

VI.

that bruise
       and the bump on my head
             were the remnants of you
             that faded the fastest

i'm ashamed to say
       how long it's taking
             to dig your voice
             out of my veins

VII .

dawn dries
the tears from my face
while i swallow what feels like
the millionth
new beginning

and today's newborn sun
casts a shadow of
my former self stretching
out behind me like
a tell-tale path
several shades off but
stuck to the soles of
my feet, nonetheless

it invites every
wayward pilgrim to trace
my renegade silhouette
through the years

only to find this woman,
face dimmed into fire's embers
because she cannot shake
her dark side from her shoes

VIII .

there are some loves
so passionate
they burn
to turn
to ash

had ours have been a fish
it would have found
a way to drown
itself

IX .

i swallowed you whole
like forbidden fruit
and the seeds of you
planted something wild
and strange in me

ACT SIX

The sky is wearing the dark like a clumsy ink blot tonight and our heroine—though, she would never call herself that—is staring at two perfect golden hairs curling around her fingers like a weak embrace.

She would be lying if she said she hadn't been hoping in some dark corner of her that he would come back. She thinks to herself, her lips still alight from his kiss, that perhaps she has only herself to blame. Perhaps all this writing was just an elaborate summoning of him. The way all art screams into the world.

I am here. I exist. And I don't need your love to be beautiful, but heaven, how I want it.

Her eyes cloud over, hot and wet. She doesn't know what else she expected to do with him once he returned. Did she really think she was going to be the one to leave the second time around? A steel smile curls up the corner of her lips before they can even think of trembling. She attempts a brittle laugh, but it breaks into awkward shards in her mouth. She swallows them.

The seconds crawl by like they've been wounded and it's all they can do to bleed a trail across the floor. Her heart takes its time between short, staccato beats—like every knock against her chest is its own desperate, feeble endeavor. It shouldn't be this hard. It should never be this hard. Not for her. Not for anyone. She feels the vindictive cruelty of it all welling up in her eyes, but before the tears can cut their way down her face—before she even knows what she is doing—she is thundering to her desk, hairs in hand. She is wrenching a dollar store sewing kit from a drawer of uncategorized clutter.

If this is all she's been cheated into, if this is the only magic she gets, then so be it. But it's magic, nonetheless. And she's not giving it up without a fight. If anyone wants her to, they can come and cut it out of her themselves. But until someone does, everything she touches is going to brush up against enchantment. She'll make sure of that.

Sitting down beside her writing, she turns on the desk lamp, as bright as it will go. She places one of the hairs carefully onto a stack of ink-smeared stories. The other she threads painstakingly through a needle. She takes a few steadying breaths, then unfurls the fist of her free hand trembling open before her. With the other hand, she plunges the needle into its open palm—catches the scream between her teeth. She had expected it to hurt, but not like this. Still, she continues, stabbing stitch after stitch across her palm. The lines tracking their way across in scarlet-soaked fortunes. The pain is striking up her arm like lightning. But she doesn't stop. She even manages a grit-toothed smile when her blood drips and dapples scarlet beads onto the pages of prose beneath her. She'd poured everything else she had into them. Why not her blood as well?

She tells herself "just one more stitch" more times than she can count. But it keeps her going. Keeps her believing that when she gets older than she can ever imagine herself being, she's going to have something to show for it. Something more than a life whisked right by her, and the question of why she did nothing but simply survive it. She's going to grit her pain hard between her teeth and work this needle across her palm, even if it kills her. Because then, at least, she'll have died for *something*.

When she has finished, she threads the next hair through the needle, shifts it to the opposite hand, and gets to work.

∞

Not a week later, the skin has barely closed over the wounds, and it begins. Slowly. In small things that could almost pass as simply strange. Some of the passersby wonder what sort of purpose sets her to striding down the street. Others just wonder what gives her the right to walk as though the very pavement was made to carry her to something greater than this. She reaches out her hand to pay for her beer, and the bartender catches a thrill of a shock in her fingers. The soap maker at the farmers' market says her hands look as though they're bursting at the seams with all they could do.

She comes to believe this, in turn. It's not easy, but she does it. There is, after all, magic in her hands. Maybe there always was. The point is, it's there now. It's coaxing ink across paper in words that shape her heart. It's lighting up the lines of her tattered script with enchantment as she traces her fingers across them in the theatre wings. It's painting her new lover's smile with supernatural every time she takes his face in her hands.

Yes, she finds love again. In time. Love like an adventure, but the trusting kind. The kind that lets her watch her secrets place their heads on his shoulders. Love like the best art. Like letting all the versions of you out at last.

At night, she lays her head against her own acceptance, and moon after moon, she teaches herself how to dream again.

It's not easy, but she manages. By heaven, how she manages!

I .

to the devil with
learning to dance in the rain
i laced tempests
through my bones
swallowed all the lightning
that bit at my boldness,
then called down
my own personal chorus of thunder,
so every storm
that came my way
knew straightaway
i wasn't going quietly

II .

perhaps you felt cheated
because i turned out
to be ten times the
woman you bargained for

i'm worth my salt
and it tastes like
stories you've never
dreamed of

III .

what if it's
a matter of forgiving
myself for all the springs
i never quite blossomed into

'cause what if this season,
true to its name,
is going to carousel its way
back around to me in time

and what if my heart
is not so much sinking
as it is dancing

    dipping
    tripping its way
        to the toes of me
           so it can whisper my feet
           forward with the words

"just be brave
for
one step longer,
love?"

IV.

my God,
my heart clenches
into a fist for fear
of losing
all You've
bloomed in it

so teach me
to pray as poetry
could only dream to

i cannot help but see stars
in the darkest night
of my soul
if you sing to me
of heaven

V.

we're all just
porcelain bones dipped
in a prayer and
there's no telling
what's going to break us

so i've come to
hold my life lightly
in my
hands

'cause all these feelings

of futility

have so heavied
my head, that the weight
of all this empty

could snap

my neck

at

any

moment

VI .

never tell yourself
that because love can conquer all
it has earned the right to reduce
china plates into confetti shards
or shake a house into rubble

do not excuse the smell of smoke,
saying to yourself that some loves
simply burn so bright that every word
cannot help but spit sparks
darling, recognize an inferno
when you see one
then run like hell

VII .

i want to stop
making all these apologies
into armor when i have
no reason to be sorry

i want to bear my thoughts,
my opinions,
my story
in all their beautiful
fragility

i want to soak my story
in any voice
but whiskey
'cause i only talk my
loudest when i wish
no one was listening

i want to pour myself into
the softest sheets and
rub the words
"i will learn to love you
as God does"
over my skin

i want films
to stop making women
look so beautiful
after they have been
raped,
beat up,
or hit by a car

i want to find
someone who says
"i love you"
for reasons other
than hearing it back

i want all my mad,
wild daring to drown out
my voice until my lips forget
how to make the shape
of "realistic"

i want to give a voice
to every poor soul who
deserves so much more
than my ego
in their throat

i want to
unfold myself
over miles of unknown
growing all the while

VIII .

tonight,
i say we host
a dinner party for our demons

i want to follow your scars like streets
like i know home is waiting
at the end of them

IX .

i know there are stories in your bones
that you would kill to learn

i know you are just learning
to let yourself be tired
so do not fear the cricks
and cracks of you
that is the sound
of a house well-loved
        well-learned
        well-lived

finally asking its ghosts
to come out (of hiding) for tea

so take out that knife you always carry,
and use it to spread your guard
across a slice of toast
then eat all your bitter-scarred words

until your tongue rises like new bread
with a voice that tastes
more like safe
this time around

X .

we tuck the night
into a spellbound dawn
and pack each other's secrets
into the bags beneath our eyes

and somewhere on the way to
sunrise, i lost my lonely
in your trust

XI .

strange, it's as if
you walked so carefully
through every heartbreak i
pulled from broken glass
and trembling lips,
gathered up all the love
i placed in fumbling hands,
and brought it all back to me

so, i am
all the more sorry
for the bruises
that are itching
to bloom up our story

some days
i just burn to go
smashing into anything
that's beautiful enough
to break
and i swear,

when i first felt
safety on your skin,
the shock of it
nearly snapped
my fingers in half

XII .

you're the last of my
spectacular beast loves

the very last crushing
velvet affair
that i, however hesitantly,
lay my heart against

whether that's because i will let you
cuff yourself 'round my ring finger
or because all the men after you will be
sturdy as the spines of books
that no one cares to open—well…
no one can quite say

        but it's the way
        you can always pull
        the truth from my tongue
        that makes me think

perhaps, just maybe,
i could tattoo my words
the color of forever
for you

XIII .

i have only
just begun to believe
in the worlds packed
into my windows

and they are begging me
to come out, so they can
sew wings onto my back

ACT SEVEN

He goes looking for her, of course. Her absence claws at his all-too-quiet days. He misses her deliberate—almost frantic—purpose, drenching everything she did. The silence is screaming louder than she ever could.

He tries to drown out the empty space she left. She was just another dreamer. And there are plenty of those. Everyone knows that. He takes up with a pretty, young thing. Churns a hit song out of her throat in weeks. But there is no thrill to it. No desperate life soaking through the walls of their expensively shabby studio apartment.

He simply cannot bring himself to hang
another song on her lips like cheap costume
jewelry.

So he goes on his way.

Now, he scours the aisles of each library and
bookstore, the audiences of every theatre,
every cabaret, every opera house. His alabaster
expression carved into something he is still
ashamed to call "longing." He is searching
all the spellbound faces for her tear-slicked
yearning. Night after night, he is listening for
a soul bashing savage against a fear-tight chest.

But he hears nothing.

Sees no one.

He never thinks to look for her on the spines
of the books. Or the stages themselves,

drenched in light. And wonder. And all her wild selves, joining hands across all the lives she learned to chase.

Her never sees her. Never saw her. Not for what she was: magic with skin on

But she does. She has learned to, at last. And this knowledge shines through her like a new name.

she is only just learning
to speak for her dreams
and her voice sounds like
starlight with teeth

ACKNOWLEDGEMENTS

Simply put, this book would not have seen the light of day if not for a great number of people—more devoted sources of support than any author deserves, really. In fact, these acknowledgements are the part of this book that I have put off for *as long as possible*, because I know I will likely forget at least one of those people, and I am dreading it. No matter how many lists of thanks-worthy individuals I've made over the last six months, how many times I have proofed them, or how many chai lattes I have siphoned to calm myself, I can't shake the feeling that *someone* has been left out. This is what happens when an overwhelming number of individuals work to turn your dreams into a reality. But now the deadline for turning in these acknowledgements is uncomfortably close—closer than I should have ever let it come. Literally, everything else is done, and I have to get these in so my layout designer has an accurate page count before we go to print. So, I'm gonna take a swig of yet another chai and try to get through this. If I *have* left you out, please accept my sincerest apologies.

This is the part where I thank God and try not to sound like an absolute tool while doing it. I'm incredibly nervous, A) because I have seen plenty of people who exhibit tool-like qualities doing just this, and B) how the blazes do you fit a Deity so extraordinarily huge into the back pages of a dinky, little indie book? I'm not one of those people who thinks any measure of success or attention is indicative of "getting in okay" with God, and I don't necessarily think He pre-destined me to write this book. That said, I have Him to thank for its story—since, as I'm sure by now, you've picked up on the semi-autobiographical tone—and I will never be able to thank Him enough. I'm so grateful for His redemption, for His hope, for Him never giving up on me, and for Him sending fragments of His love pouring out of the mouths, hands, and lives of so many people around me— many of whom will find their names below.

...Is this starting to sound like a sermon to a captive audience? I hope not. Those make my blood boil. So, let's move on now to my fellow human beings, shall we?

When I was broke and seriously doubting my ability as a writer, I had managed to save enough money for a BIG author's conference in New York. I was in desperate need of some professional guidance, and thrilled to go soak up all the knowledge this event had to offer. Then I had some severe car trouble, and all the conference money went toward my little Hyundai, shortly before the registration date. The following rock stars raised the funds I needed to attend, despite my car woes. And they did it in less than a week!

-Melanie Dosen, who told me I had twelve hours to start a GoFundMe or she would do it for me, then was one of the first people to bravely throw money at my crazy. Thanks for that. Best. Threat. Ever.

-Jonathan and Joelle Barnett, you two are utter joys. Thank you for taking notice of this, and then taking the time to feed the dream.

-Allison Fode, fire and ice all the way. Love you, lady.

-Jeremy McDaniel, it has been such a thrill watching you thrive. Thank you for your constant faith in me to do the same, dear friend.

-Sarah Simpson, I'm pretty sure you are the human embodiment of hot chocolate (often with a kick.) I never get tired of hearing what goes on in your incredible mind, and I don't think you'll ever realize how much I admire you.

-Sean Townsend, you are magic, through and through. Thank you for your tireless encouragement. For reading more of my poems than I think anyone else has. For sharing your own wild and wondrous creations with me. And for all the handwritten letters. I count my life so much richer for having you in it.

-Megan Moore-Jensen, keep tracking your glorious brand of whimsy all over the place.

-Nikki Looper, thank you for being one of the first people to read my work—and for putting so much thought and excitement into it. Thank you for talking about the characters I created as though you knew them as personal friends. That meant more than I will ever be able to say.

-Maylin Tu, a fearless powerhouse of a writer. Here's to you.

-Katie Welch, the roommate I have lived with for the longest, who never once made me feel guilty when I would display antisocial tendencies.

-Melissa Dorman and Amanda Rapinchuk, master cat wranglers and better cooks than I will ever be. I miss our family dinners and subsequent conversations, but I hope Portland is treating you well.

-Laurel Bennett, a formidable force of a woman. My gosh, the world is SO lucky to have you, and I get to hear all your hilarious stories as you make it better! Thank you for always being there to listen to me, to pray, and to pour the wine.

-Ashley Crosby, I'm a little embarrassed to say this, but the consistent respect and admiration I had for you as an artist made me almost disproportionately excited when I saw you had contributed to this cause.

-Heather Crowley, my goodness, am I happy to have met you! Thank you for ensuring that my bookshelves are well and tastefully stocked.

-Joel Gonzaga, you're a credit to house Slytherin. *tips hat*

-Ryan Luchessi, you are a fairy godfather—only with angel wings, because I sincerely doubt whether this earth actually deserves you.

-David Crowley, who contributed funds, and then personally made his sumptuous grilled cheese sandwiches for the highest donors. Also, thank you, thank you, thank you for not only telling me that I really needed to stop working three jobs at once so I could have time to write, but for actually getting me a job that enabled me to do just that.

-Whitney and Jason Smales/Ata, you two are the exact kind of friends that everyone needs. Thank you for your continuous thoughtfulness, for caring so intently for my ambitions, and for all the inspiration you have provided to me through the years—both by the internet and by mail.

-Daniel Matas, my platonic soul mate, who (among so many other things) came to New York with me so I could have moral support, and so the two of us could have an adventure.

So, thank you, donors. I know all of you are probably slightly confused as to how I went into this conference with a middle-grade fantasy novel, and now, years later, there's this magical realism poetry collection/story to show for it.* Just rest assured that you made it happen and that I am more grateful than I can say. You got me to the event that started this process, and you gave me so much confidence—showing me that people had enough faith in my writing to actually (and very tangibly) invest in it. That meant the world to me.

To my online community of followers (both Facebook and Instagram), you gals and guys rock my socks off! It was the strangest thing, putting out scraps of my soul into the internet void, then waiting and wondering what would come of it. Never did I imagine that the answer would be you lot. Thank you for accepting such deep and strange parts of me with open arms. Thank you for the countless messages and comments. Thank you for all the music/movie/book suggestions. Thank you for counseling me through that especially bad haircut, then providing me with pictures and ideas of how I could fix it. Thank you for following me throughout all this, for taking the time to tell me how my writing touched you personally, and especially for trusting me enough to share your own stories with me. You are exactly the kind of audience that just about every writer hopes they'll get. And I'm so happy to have you along for the ride.

To Julie Guzzetta and Kimberly Ito, editors extraordinaire, thank you, ladies, for lending your expertise to this work, for seeing exactly where it wanted to go, and for making sure that it got there.

Alysia Harris, working with you on this book was a dream come true—Seriously, it took consistent effort not to fan girl all over you. A thousand thanks for your spectacular eye and priceless input.

Madeline Crowley, thank you for my gorgeous cover and the stunning layout. And for answering so many of the questions I had for my first go at slaying the book beast. You were a consistent source of information and wisdom, going truly above and beyond.

Sarah Shreves, thank you for the gorgeous author photo. The way you genuinely invest in others as individuals absolutely shows in your work, and I'm so glad I finally got an excuse to do a shoot with you. (I'd been wanting one for years.)

Infinite thanks to Chris Slaney, the best non-biological brother a girl could ask for. And to the rest of the Lovelies for their perpetual enthusiasm.

To the Five, for putting up with me for so long.

Jessica Nicholas and Kristina Giblin, it has occurred to me that I have been referring to both of you kindred spirits as my book doulas. Because there seems to be no other term for what you have been doing throughout this process. And you have each been killing it, by the way.

Katie Elsaesser, thank you for reading my work with Nikki all those years ago, and for getting excited enough to imagine backstories, and to ask for prequels and sequels. That was, without question, one of the best nights of my life. It was the first time ever that I began to think I could actually do this. Thank you for assuring me over and over again that this was indeed what I was supposed to be doing, for accompanying me to multiple poetry slams, and for letting me come over to your place on my lunch breaks when I was working by you and really needed it.

On that note, thanks to all the work places who knew full well I was writing on the clock and chose not to fire me.

To the churches, Ecclessia and Radius, thank you for creating such safe spaces where people can take out the deepest parts of themselves and look them over. I can say with confidence that that not only made (and continues to make) me a better writer, but a much better person.

To the ladies of Faith Played Out, your fearless acceptance of honesty made it so much easier to tell my own messy truths in this project. Thank you.

To my family, Mom, Dad, Nick, and the big, fat extended one, thank you so much for putting up with my weird. For buying me fishnets and combat boots, for keeping me well-fed, and for listening to me, even when we don't agree. Thanks for letting me be a little weirdo, even before you knew it was going to amount to anything. I'm sure it got quite scary, wondering just what I was going to do with myself.

And a special thank you to Rebekah, who diligently raided the library with me, summer after summer. When I said you were a great part of the reason I started writing, I meant it wholeheartedly. Thank you for buying me candy to eat while I listened to you read (with SO much animation.) Thank you for using sheets to turn our bunk bed into a pirate ship, and thank you for letting me be the captain. As far as big sisters go, you're tops. Always will be.

Robert, I have said this many times, and I'll say it again—only this time in print, for everyone to read: This book is here because of you. Thank you for tirelessly working to realize my crazy dreams, even when I would tell you not to. I can't believe we did this. Heck, I still can't believe I get you. There simply aren't enough words for how much I love you, but by the end of a lifetime, I may be able to give you some idea. So, thanks for, you know, marrying me so I could have the chance to do that.

And finally, to you, the reader of this book (and apparently, of the acknowledgements, as well. Major points for dedication!) I'm not sure how you got these words of mine in your hands, but I'm awfully glad you did! Thank you for taking a walk in my stories. I hope you found yourself in there somewhere.

---

*See, what happened was this: I took said novel to said conference, and two specific lectures really stuck with me. One lecture about structure, in which they told us that every chapter should, in a way, be able to stand on its own, structurally, like a short story; and one lecture by a widely known and contagiously exuberant poet that made me greatly miss the craft poetry. So, by the end of said conference, I was writing short stories for practice in chapter structure and cranking out poems again, wondering why I had ever stopped doing so. Then I started putting lines from some of the poems online. Then this book appeared.

Printed in Poland
by Amazon Fulfillment
Poland Sp. z o.o., Wrocław

50479356R00087